DEPARTURE

Other titles from Central Square Press

A HARD SUMMATION by Afaa Michael Weaver

CRACKED CALABASH by Lisa Pegram

THE NEXT VERSE POETS MIXTAPE - VOLUME ONE: The 4 x 4
by Melanie Henderson, Fred Joiner, Lisa Pegram, Enzo Silon Surin

FEAR OF DOGS & OTHER ANIMALS by Shauna M. Morgan

A LETTER OF RESIGNATION: AN AMERICAN LIBRETTO
by Enzo Silon Surin

LETTERS FROM CONGO by Danielle Legros Georges

DEPARTURE

poems

Samuel Miranda

CENTRAL SQUARE PRESS

Copyright © 2017 by Samuel Miranda.

All rights reserved. No part of this book may be used or reproduced in any manner whatsoever without written permission from the publisher, except in the case of brief quotations embodied in critical articles or reviews.

All inquiries and permissions requests should be addressed to the Publisher:

Central Square Press
Lynn, Massachusetts

publisher@centralsquarepress.com
www.centralsquarepress.com

Printed in the United States of America
First Edition

ISBN-13: 978-1-941604-06-9

ISBN-10: 1-941604-06-4

Cover art: "Abrazo en la Calle Neptuno" by Samuel Miranda & Lazaro Batista

Book design: Enzo Silon Surin

*For my grandfather Antonio Gines
who did not say much but left me so many stories to tell,
and my students who pushed a quiet man to find the power in words.*

*And to the DC writer's community who has nurtured my voice and
always called me to task.*

CONTENTS

Three-Cent Version, Part 1 – Fur-Collared *Diosa* from Ponce   3

Three-Cent Version, Part 2 – Man with His Hat Tipped Just Right   4

Casa Evita   6

Sestina: Abuela   8

¿Por qué te Vas?   10

Sobreviviente: Paradelle for a Survivor   11

Departure 1   13

Departure 2   14

Departure 3   15

Departure 4   16

Departure 5   17

Abrazo en la Calle Neptuno   18

Ghazals for Departure

    The Erotic   20

    The Comic   21

    The Pathetic   22

    The Furious   23

The Heroic	24
The Terrible	25
The Odious	26
The Marvelous	27

Notes   29
About the Author   31

departure

Three-Cent Version

    in conversation with *La Playa Negra I* by Antonio Martorrell

Version 1 – Fur-Collared Diosa from Ponce

This is the three-cent version of me.
Three cents ain't easy to come by
and it doesn't include the price
of the photo, the envelope, or the paper.

Pero pal carajo, it's worth it
since I get to send you a picture
of who I want you to see me as.
Out here *en los nueva yores*.
I am, the fur-collared *diosa* from Ponce

I take this picture on the tar
of a rooftop that the sun heats,
to the point where it reminds me of home.

But this ain't home.
Tomorrow I am back
to the woman you don't ever get to see,
the callous-fingered seamstress from *la* 116,
whose fingers have become accustomed to the
sensation of silk she can't afford
to sew into her own bodice.

Three-Cent Version

    in conversation with *La Playa Negra II* by Antonio Martorrell

Version 2 - Man with His Hat Tipped Just Right

This is the three-cent version of me
hat tipped just right
black shoes
fading into the black
of tar that lines a beach
waters never seem to find their way to.
From up here I can view the city
and become who I want you to see.
Tomorrow you will be tempted,
like a thousand others to ride the Marine Tiger
and come and be the me I send via air mail.

Tomorrow I go back to me,
the bootblack who snaps the rhythm
of a mambo, played Palladium style
with my cloth, against shoe leather
until it is buffed to a high shine
and ready to enter the spaces
where I am never welcome.

So welcome to the tar beaches
and the laborers' hands, and a life

where the three-cent versions
of a people fly home the lies,
of a living less beautiful
than the man
in the hat that is tipped just right
or the woman
with the fur collar
wrapped around her neck.

Casa Evita

> in conversation with *Casa Evita*, Hiram Maristany

The pentecostal minister warns,
evita la del piso 5, Espiritista.
Look at how she stands
at the window, arms crossed
pillow waiting for her
to lean onto the ledge
and call up her next victim.

A curse is waiting on you there,
you can smell the devil
from down the hall
just behind the scent of urine
that's been soaked up
by tiled hallways and brick walls.

In Casa Evita a *gabán* for papa
or a *guayabera*,
something that he can put on
when he stands on the rooftop
that will make him look
like the dollars he earns stretch far enough
to fill an empty fridge.

In *Mi Tienda* a bata to send *Mamita*.
A housedress, covered in palm fronds
that she will wear as she sweeps
the sidewalk in front of the cement house
her sons built for her
with money earned in a city
where weeds take root in cement
but palms are just paintings
on the *bodegas* roll down gates.

When sound breaks loose
It looks for the open window
makes the curtains choose
between a bugaloo's swing
and that step the horn section
of a good salsa tune makes you take.
They always choose the horns.

Sestina: Abuela

Abuela's tejada floats before slowly blinding eyes
and the young man sitting in the chair is visiting
a wandering mind that wakes at 4am and sees
the early morning as afternoon. It is age
that defines the visions. Sleeping alone
makes dreams and the company in them real.

Abuela believed that demons were real.
When she kneeled to pray she always kept her eyes
open. The first time the devil came to visit she was alone.
He told her he loved visiting
the saintly, when they were at a sinning age
and death was a thing they could see.

Grandpa believes the things he sees
are messages. They may not be real
but they come from *abuela*. Age
confuses demons with wives. The eyes
see those they wish were visiting.
His wife or the devil: either one beats being alone.

Grandpa used to walk the length of Manhattan alone,
searching for bargains. In his mind he sees

Canal Street or Delancey, remembers visiting
Julio the barber. Give him scissors and real
magic was done. He always had the hair cut away from the eyes.
That way you couldn't lie to him, not even about your age.

Grandpa feels that at his age
he shouldn't be left alone.
He complains that his hair is in his eyes
and that it causes him to misinterpret what he sees.
He thinks the *tejadas* are real,
but who is the young man who is always visiting?

Grandpa is always visiting
the restroom. Peeing is something he does a lot at his age.
The young man who seems real
understands and waits in the bedroom. Alone
in the bathroom he sees
the roaches scurrying and closes his eyes.

Abuela always closed her eyes, denying that roaches came visiting.
There were things she didn't want to see. That didn't change with age.
Grandpa left her alone, let her believe what she wanted. He
knows the roaches are real.

¿Por Qué Te Vas?

In a small house made of cement
the cane cutter's children
became men and women
who departed, and when asked
"¿Por qué te vas?" avoided the eyes.

They packed the small suitcases
that poverty supplied the contents for.
Suited up in their best
they boarded a Pan-Am flight
waking in *los Nueva Yores*
to the song of sewing
and the hum of machines
that made their dance faster
than the one farms and cane fields taught them.

They sent their images back to those who stayed
standing behind pedestals that declared *"Te Quiero"*
or on rooftops, cityscapes behind them
that said I am more,
but did not acknowledge how little they had.

Upon receipt
the cane cutter would sit on his porch
open the air-mail envelope

and wish them back,
wanting children he could touch,
rather than the images
that reminded him of empty rooms.

In time empty rooms became an empty house
that did not mourn absence
but crumbled under the weight of vacancy.

Sobreviviente: **Paradelle for a Survivor**
in conversation with the work of Adrian Roman

What happens to a home that will not sell,
What happens to a home that will not sell,
as the neighbors sit and watch it slumber?
as the neighbors sit and watch it slumber?
Sit as it happens, and watch what the neighbors sell
slumber, to a home that will not.

She will not sit quiet with the memory.
She will not sit quiet with the memory.
She will comb the stories from her hair.
She will comb the stories from her hair.
She sits, will not quiet the stories with comb,
she wills memory from her hair.

Her gray is survival,
Her gray is survival,
she smiles through their departure.
she smiles through their departure.
Through her gray, departure smiles,
she is their survival.

The neighbors sell, she smiles through their departure.
She is survival, will not slumber, not sit quiet
as she wills memory from gray hair.
Watch her comb through her stories to home.

Departure 1

This is what remains,
eyes that have watched
how departure returns.

Departure 2

The stories have been stored
in wrinkles, deepened
by the exodus of youth.

Departure 3

Those who stay
sit on gated porches,
locking the exits.

Departure 4

Empty houses
are for sale, memories
get lost in the transaction.

Departure 5

The cats have invaded the porch,
decorating it with their leavings.
Everything else is gone.

Abrazo en la Calle Neptuno

A long flight of steps climbed.
The slap of rubber-soled shoes on stone.
The sound of too many years,
of not enough visits.

At the top, a mother
stands enclosed,
in a space too long
empty of a son's voice.

Arriving, a son
encloses his mother
in an embrace,
that holds miles and years
inside it. They stay here
wrapped loosely
in each other's arms
afraid that tightening
would crush the days he has
into hours, never enough.

Ghazals for Departure
after the eight sentiments of the Natyashastra

The Erotic

When I placed the garland of white flowers around her neck
the petals looked out of place and garish around her neck.

When she left, she left with a single adornment, a scarf
white silk she wraps loosely around the dark skin of her neck.

White silk has turned to snake, spitting the venom of desire,
she is unsure how long she must live with this burden around her neck.

A thousand heads have sprouted, how can she control this, desire
is not the softness of silk or the scent of white flowers around her neck.

The white petals are words spoken softly, that recount a departure
and sting like thorns pushed into the flesh around her neck.

Her limbs become light as petals and sway, giving in to desires
that dance like a lover's fingers traveling the distance around her neck.

She has donned a dress the color of moss, it hangs loosely on her frame
its movements match her breath, only the collar is tight around her neck.

Her breathing slows, and she sighs her need, unfulfilled desire
which she wears like a garland of white flowers around her neck.

The Comic

This is how you move around a god, understand his rhythms and dance. Make sure your feet don't falter, let your laughter match the dance.

Your true nature pushes against the walls you have built to keep it hidden. Walls crash, you echo with a HA! HA! HA! arms bending into your dance.

You dare flare your nose, release laughter so heavy it bends head into shoulders. Tears in your eyes, shoulders and head shaking, you begin a trembling dance.

You quiet the vulgarity of your laughter, and find your smile again, as you open narrowed eyes, hands taking hold of your sides, you re-choreograph your dance.

You try to change your status, control the laughter that is pouring from you. You hide your teeth, let eyes bloom, newly opened flowers whose petals dance.

Is this who you want to be, controlled, passions quarantined, a dancer unworthy of your limbs, or one with the freedom to entice others to join your furious dance?

Laugh loudly, let the gods hear you, let them know you aren't ashamed to laugh at them, that your eyes have been opened wide by the release of your laughter. You control the dance.

Now you are who you need to be, not the gentle laughter of a breeze, not the simple smile of a polite introduction. You're the laughter of storm, where rain and wind become the dance.

The Pathetic

Tell me, what causes the tears? Is it the need for departure?
You kneel and pray for respite, this will not delay your departure.

There are many ways to leave, each one a different sorrow you will carry.
There's no returning, though your heartbeat tries to overwhelm the need for departure.

Your cries are heard at your destination, announcing your loss,
but no one can feel the weight of limbs pulled down by departure.

You stand at the edge of a sea, exile pulling the breath from your lungs.
Air doesn't wish to enter you, it knows that you'll just hasten its departure.

You watch the crows. Black and silent they know what leaving feels like
they know that you must weigh your sins, and then welcome departure.

You faint before the noose that hangs in wait, the executioner is patient.
You will not feel the tightening of rope yet, will not know death as departure.

The Furious

I wrap feet in strips of burial clothes so I can remember why I travel.
I watched others leave until their bodies became a distance to travel.

I pound my chest driving away the demons of silence brought by departure,
each slap marking the tempo that my feet will keep as I travel.

My feet are wrapped tightly but I do not slide them into shoes.
I want the soles to feel the road, to blister, to be cut by the miles I travel.

I do not want to leave, this is not a road I have chosen to follow
This is an exile demanded by guns and bombs, so I must travel.

There is no need for you to describe loss, I revisit that image daily.
It has helped me map the road that will pull the breath from me as I travel.

This road is not a place you return from, not a place to believe in
I have left belief behind with the carcass of a home that bid me travel.

The Heroic

The elephant's hurried step can be heard as thunder, listen. You are the one who is elephant, meant to thunder, listen.

You have taken to the bottle and given in to the sound of thunder. To how it grows stronger with each sip, drink and listen.

You let yourself be crushed by the weight of your surrender but you are promised new life, so you bid your spirit, listen.

Each morning you welcome your resurrection, breath, a life brought back from the dead to hit the bottle and do battle, listen.

They appear before you, your enemies, in armor, emboldened. They don't hear you cast your net, they did not learn to listen.

You hear the voices of the dead light up your ears, lightning that with each strike adds a note, there is the song, listen.

Will you pour a sip from your bottle, let it pour into the blood of the fallen? They have sacrificed their song. Will you listen?

The Terrible

They remind you of owls, the crying children that are here with you, imprisoned. Those who hold you, ignore your pleas for their release. They will remain imprisoned.

You are not bound but there is no freedom here, with each step she takes, your child creates a circle around you, builds a wall so you won't wander, so you'll remain imprisoned.

You sit listening for the owl cries of the children to stop ringing in your ears, watch your child circle. You wish to be free of it all. Free even, of memory. How long will you remain imprisoned?

The sound of the ocean used to be calming, used to be what you walked towards, used to be where you swallowed your child's laughter, until the boat, until the sea. You remain imprisoned

by the memory of children's bodies floating, soundless, their owl cries swallowed by the salt of a sea hands pulled you from, unaware this action would cause you to remain imprisoned.

There is no escaping how memory becomes nightmare, becomes visits from the dead. The dead who bring your child with them so you will remember that beside them she will remain imprisoned.

Remember that the sea, like your exile, will offer an embrace that will give the appearance of safety. That the sea, like your sorrow, will always taste of salt. That in grief, you will always remain imprisoned.

The Odius

What are the things that make your hands tremble?
Not the pleasures, though these too can make your body tremble.

Is it the crunch of bodies, desperate for departure?
How they crowd onto a train and sway like cargo as it trembles.

Is it the ocean's need to surge against the sides of a boat
pushing until you vomit out the last vestiges of home and tremble?

Is it simply the stillness of a body, stiffened by the fear of arrival,
by not knowing whether to cry or run, whether to rejoice or tremble?

Is it the disgust of those who greet you, who see you as driftwood
or spume pushed ashore by an ocean that exiled you, as your body trembled?

Is it the fainting of a child who has been denied home, as others bend heads
walking by as if she were invisible, but still cover their noses and tremble?

What are the things that make you shake your limbs, that make you want
to rid yourself of their mark, spit out their bitterness, and tremble?

The Marvelous

Your eyes are opened wide, they stare at a sky full of stars
Are the constellations a single entity or a multitude of stars?

The heavens seem to tremble if you stare long enough.
Do your eyes see the couples dancing in the brightness of the stars?

Do Orion and Cassiopeia listen to boleros filling the space between them?
Do they grab hold when no one is watching and dance or are they just stars?

Is this a magic trick, an illusion that plays with your position
in relation to the night sky, making you see more than just stars?

Does the sight of the north star fill you with fear, make you think
departure will be necessary, make you close your eyes to banish the stars?

Or do you welcome the beauty of an open ocean, and the sky
made brighter by the presence of constellations, telling the story of the stars?

Is this your story, one where a darkness is filled only with the light
of small dots spread over the miles you must travel, a road of stars?

Notes

1. *Three Cent Version*, *Version 1* and *2*, *Casa Evita*, and *Sobreviviente* were all conversations with Puerto Rican visual artists whose work document the Puerto Rican Diaspora and the effects of the exodus that occurred in the 40s and 50s, which has seen a resurgence in the last few years and is now amplified by the effects of Hurricane Maria.

2. *Ghazals for Departure* are influenced by the Natyashastra a treatise on the performing arts by Bharata Muni. The poems use the eight sentiments identified and explained in the text, as a way to discuss the modern issues around forced migration.

about the author

Samuel Miranda grew up in the South Bronx and has made his home in Washington, DC. He is a visual artist, poet and teacher who uses his craft to highlight the value of everyday people and places. His work has been heavily influenced by Puerto Rican culture and family history, as well as his interactions with the people in his city, his students, and people he encounters in his travels.